Dear Almost

Barataria Poetry
Ava Leavell Haymon, Series Editor

ALSO BY
MATTHEW THORBURN

Subject to Change

Disappears in the Rain

Every Possible Blue

This Time Tomorrow

A Green River in Spring

Louisiana State University Press

Baton Rouge

Dear Almost

a poem

MATTHEW THORBURN

Published by Louisiana State University Press
Copyright © 2016 by Matthew Thorburn
All rights reserved
Manufactured in the United States of America
LSU Press Paperback Original
First printing

Designer: Michelle A. Neustrom
Typeface: Miller Text
Printer and binder: LSI

Library of Congress Cataloging-in-Publication Data

Names: Thorburn, Matthew, author.
Title: Dear almost : a poem / Matthew Thorburn.
Description: Baton Rouge : Louisiana State University Press,
    [2016]
Identifiers: LCCN 2016005786| ISBN 978-0-8071-6431-0
    (pbk. : alk. paper) | ISBN 978-0-8071-6432-7 (pdf) | ISBN
    978-0-8071-6433-4 (epub) | ISBN 978-0-8071-6434-1
    (mobi)
Classification: LCC PS3620.H76 A6 2016 | DDC 811/.6—dc23
    LC record available at http://lccn.loc.gov/2016005786

The paper in this book meets the guidelines for permanence
and durability of the Committee on Production Guidelines for
Book Longevity of the Council on Library Resources. ∞

Deep in a life / is another life.

—Marianne Boruch, "Nest"

Contents

Once in Early Spring

Winter's so long I forget
what spring is like
until a weird crackle makes me
duck and look up—
a dingy gray, a flash of light,
that cardinal just touched
red along her edges,
a shiny stripe
of clear packing tape flickering
from her beak. This
morning's banner slaps
past her breast. Maybe
eight inches, maybe a foot?
And about as heavy
as she is: one-ounce wish.
So that her flight is
flighty, a hop and flap
flutter skip from
branch to branch to
lower branch—here-ing
and there-ing—then
the branch dips

and she's off again,
down to the top of the chain-
link fence. But it tangles
her feet, ticks against her
wings—*crick, crack*—
meaning what
this Sunday morning?
A sign? Or just to say
she can't really fly with it
but won't
give it up, this panel of light.
But for what? A window

or waterproofing or
what sort of nesty home
repair? *What cheer cheer cheer*
she doesn't sing
or tell me why. She'd have to

unlock her beak, let it go,
learn to talk.
What's in the front yard
she wants
in the back. But don't we all?
Never enough, never
just right. This is what
spring is like:
work to do. We want
more. Another morning

alone at my desk, wondering
about you, my window
open to what may come—
a communion of sparrows,
crows or just this
once a phoebe might alight
on the fire
escape: jittery
gray-green dash of feathers
and like a mirror
he'd call, *fee-bee, fee-bee.*
First one back
this spring: happy
to preside over everything

for five seconds,
then zip off
under this pale porcelain blue

streaked with clouds
which was once
the dark blue just shy
of black, then warmed up
slowly, like I do,
getting these early words
down in lines like
branches, first
feelers I put out to see
what feels back.

The amazing thing is not
that geese can get sucked
into an Airbus engine
and cause it to conk out
or that a pilot can tell air-
traffic control, "There's only
one thing I can do,"
then take a deep breath
and do it—ditch
in the Hudson with a buck
and whine, then walk
the aisle as the plane fills
with water to make sure
everyone's gotten out—
but that afterwards

many who weren't hurt
in a lifelong way, only
shaken, roughed up, no doubt
shocked, had nothing else
to do, finally, except take a bus
back to LaGuardia and
catch another plane home.
Amazing too how
before long people stop
talking about it, they move on
and eventually need
an extra beat to recognize

that camera-shy pilot
when he appears—retired
now, somehow *smaller*
now, no longer shy—
as an air-travel expert
("Sometimes carry-ons

just shouldn't be
carried on") on the nightly
news and connect
his name to what he did
that day, probably—
let's face it—because
no one died.
Though most stories
don't end

like that. In Shanxi
Province, the BBC told me
late last night when
I should've been asleep
beside Lily instead of
sitting up in the dark,
twenty-four workers—
all men, the reporter
said, and some much older
than I would've imagined—
were trapped
in a mile-deep mineshaft
deemed too dangerous now
for a rescue, though
apparently it was safe
enough to work in:
shovel clang and gravel
rumble turned to echoing

silence. Eventually
the company execs sent in
a slender silver robot
with tank treads, long
pincer hands, a camera
for a face, but

all it found—how long
it looked, they didn't
say—was a single miner's
helmet, dented
and dusty, its frail light
still burning.

April fifth, first clear day
after a week of rain,
so we drive north
where the county road bends
around jags of glacier-
cut rock. Sunlight knifes
through the clouds,
the radio fuzzes out
between towns.

I'm at the wheel, Lily's
got the map, her mom half-
dozes, half-dreams (of
what, I wonder, and in
which language? Chinese?
English?) in back.
We're headed into the forest
to Chuang Yen Monastery,
its orange roofs lost

in the leaves. We and others
like us—parents and
children, grandparents,
mostly Chinese
but also a few waiguoren like me—
come here for Qingming:
a good time to get out
in the sun ("Soak up
some vitamin D," my mother-
in-law advises me) and sniff
the green shoots of spring.
"Qingming" means *clear
bright*. At the monastery
it's also time to look
back: we're here

because Lily's father is here,
his ashes in an urn
in the tall granite wall
high up on a hill in the woods.
One more translation
of "Qingming?"
Tomb-sweeping day.
We've brought an apple,
an orange—the sweet
treats he loved—and sticks
of yellow incense and
paper ghost money to burn
so he will have it
where he is. Here the living
visit the dead, but first

there's food. Here I learn
to look more carefully:
some monks—heads shorn
to stubble, crinkly-eyed
behind no-nonsense
specs, in orange
robes, tire-tread sandals—
are women. The monks
serve us a lunch (is this
the food they eat
every day?) of thin yellow
curry, bean curd and bean
sprouts ladled over
steaming scoops of rice.
And then finally

we follow one another up
the gravel path—hands

on shoulders, some with canes—
to Thousand Lotus Terrace
where the ashes are
interred. We burn incense.
We put our hands together
and bow three times.
All the prayers here
are chanted in old Chinese,
a circling hum
I could drown in,
and so mean nothing to me
(or anything) as my mind
wanders off into the woods.
My own words fall

away now, sound weird,
off, odd jangle-clang
in the ear like when
we say something again
and again until
it slips loose of its mooring,
its meaning, so that
we wind up staring
or better yet, close our eyes.
Try to feel our hearts
rattle the brittle cages
of our chests—still
there, keeping
time—and so let that
show what we mean

(since you're
not here, not even
in this wall)

to those we miss and now
remember and now
miss more.
Lao Wen saw this once
or made it up, so long ago
it no longer matters:
The mourners on a misty
morning, their faces wet—
with rain or tears, I couldn't say.

    Rain or tears—
that's the grace I want
    on this sun-shot day.

Morning once more
and the birds compete
with our neighbor
Wenjing (her window
must be open too)
and her pipa, Chinese
great-grandfather to the guitar.
But the sparrows
have an edge: thrown off
by so many apartment
lights and streetlights,
by all-night TV glow and car
headlights, they
chitter-chatter round
the clock, their lungs tiny
but strong. They repeat
their songs again
and again until

they die. The pipa's
pear-shaped, held upright,
its stout neck parallel
to Wenjing's: she wraps
her arms around it
like a child. (Lily leans in
over my shoulder
to wonder, "Why do you
never see the pipa
played by a man?") Twangy
trills, pluck and strum.
Such stops and starts and
stops. Faintest string
hum. Then a flash of hand
and wrist, a bright burst
and she's off

again: rush of water
over rock, horse gallop
and warrior call, and the birds
stopped short by this
sudden theft
of the morning's attention
sit still like me, all
our mouths ajar and

wait, I know this!
Wenjing's playing "Snow
in Early Spring,"
a folk song from her
part of China—way
up north—though without
the high cry of the erhu
or the yangqin like starlight
spangling a river
to make the journey with her.
Only her pipa, a pale gull
swooping out over the water
to search for one
who was lost. *Pipa,* I told her
once—happy
to have discovered this

bit of trivia and brought it
home like a bright
scrap of tinsel—is also Spanish:
slang for *having a good time.*
We were kicked back
in folding chairs
under the oaks and slow
clouds, cold drinks in warm
hands, and yet I couldn't

help it: this perfect
moment—Wenjing's laugh, her
dentist husband Dennis's
patient smile, Lily's
laugh, her grass-green
party dress, sunlight catching
in the sun tea
pitcher—made me

antsy, made me remember
that overworked
short-story writer who longed
for more hours
to make his pencils dull
so he could sharpen them
again, who told a friend, "You
have to understand:

    having a good time
is not my idea
    of having a good time."

Speaking of words—
or *not* speaking
actually—speech pathology
is Lily's
work: what happens
when words
fail or can't be found,
when the sounds don't come
out right or
at all, the way even
now I can't talk
about you. Though grief's
not a physical
affliction like aphasia,
that sudden numbing loss

caused by a stroke or blow
to the head, crash
down the stairs, some gut-
reaction act
of bravery gone
in an instant (a gun pulled?
knife flicked out?)
horribly wrong. Or sometimes
children are just born
this way, slow
to get going, big-eyed
but silent. Or—
"there's almost always
another *or*," Lily says, "because

we're human"—
or their parents aren't
from here and so
speak another language,

Chinese or Urdu, Finnish
or Flemish, so
it just takes longer
to learn
this one. I wish you
could see her:
glasses pushed up
in her hair, Lily
sits on the hard carpet
with a once-
scared three-year-old
who's smiling, who's suddenly—

suddenly after weeks
with picture
books, with flashcards,
after weeks with
music, with games and songs
and puppets—saying
something. Maybe
the tongue doesn't know
where to go. It takes time
but you can reteach it, usually—
the brain's wiring
is sometimes re-
wire-able. Or the breath
doesn't do
its pushing or
the twisty extension cord

between brain and mouth
needs plugging back in
so that bolt
of lightning synaptic translation—
thought to electricity

to motion—can
happen:
the tongue taps
the palate: vocal chords
hum: warm
air rushes out as the soft
shy voice
we've waited
so long to hear. *When words fall*
away, I think, even
as I sharpen my pencil

since what else can I do?
I'm not a painter
or potter, not a sculptor
but someone who
works with words, re-
ordering them here
on the back of an old calendar
page (it's May;
what else can I do now
with April?), my
messy gestures made letter
by letter—*here's what*
this feels like—
so you can feel it too.

∿

But when words fall away
I can't help it: I walk back

into that dark room.
I watch what happened

happen again. Locked
in present tense: stuck

in that dark narrow room.
Goddamn dead-hum

silence floods in. I see us there
where the clock stops.

Where everything changes
before time starts unspooling

again, half speed now, and all
will always be *after:*

This morning we're holding
our breath in this
too-warm room, waiting
to "detect"—
that is the word—your
heartbeat, if you
have one. Two weeks ago
you were there
on the dark screen, smaller
than expected, but
there, but still.
"Presenting as
not viable"—those were
the cold, the heartless

words. *"Keep growing,"*
I prayed—those were
my words, forgetting how
long ago I gave up
on prayers, still
willing and pleading with
whomever might hear me
to listen, thinking if
we don't have
faith—or if not faith,
not even that,
then hope, simple hope—
then our hands
are empty. We walk
in the dark. Pale
shadow on the sonogram,
pearl button we've fastened
our deepest wish to—
we are knocking
on your wall. Please,
little heart, knock back.

The Light that Lasts
All Summer

Taking out the trash
I stop, bag in hand,
to look up at the moon—

looking up, of course,
being what real New Yorkers
supposedly *never* do
since we're too cool
and always in too big a rush,
thank you very much, though if true
this would mean we'd miss
practically everything. But here

in the northwest corner
of the Bronx—about as far
as we could go
without saying so long
to the city—all leafy
green on a high terraced hill
in the sharp elbow
of two rivers, mighty
coffee-dark Hudson
and skinny smooth Harlem,
where the mumble-grumble
of the commuter
train's just noticeable
back beyond those trees,
looking up is

what we do. Also looking out,
looking in and over and
even looking hard
at what no one wants to see:
the man collecting cans
for the five-cent

refund, his cart piled high
with garbage bags, breathing in
the sour-sweet stink
of flat Pepsi and stale beer
he can't wash away
or the grubby-fingered woman
on the 1 train asking
each of us, "Can I get a hand
up, not a hand out?"
When she turns to me I see
she's pregnant.
My moon-viewing party's
a quick one—the trash
bag's heavy, ripe, the night

crisp and shivery. I've seen
skunks and possums creep
from these woods. And once
a raccoon, slow and low-slung,
came trundling up
the hundred and fifteen steps
it takes to climb our hill
as the sun was reeling
into the sky and I was trudging
down and off to the subway,
to Manhattan, to work.
His razory claws scritch-
scratched the concrete.
I held my breath: he passed
right by. I'm remembering
trash bags, raccoons,
the steps I retrace
each morning, each night,
because I want to show you

these days and the ten
thousand things they're filled
with: dirty rivers broken
into shards of light, old oaks
and elms, Amtrak trains,
the bright surprise of Chinese
music, the erhu's plaintive cry
that makes me lonely for

someone I can't name,
dozens of sparrows gossiping
in an overgrown hedge,
unleashed dogs, coffee light
and sweet, a shouty blue jay
letting his wake-up call rip
through the morning, darkness
and starlight, the way
even during the day we can still
sometimes see the moon—

a mystery to me,
one I would've read up on
so I could explain it to you
when you wondered why too.
I want to show you
what life is like
here where you ought to be
with us, but aren't:
a not-uncommon story
though few people will tell you

it's their story too. They choose
not to relive it, relieved
not to revisit what happened

or didn't. What should have.
What went wrong
for no other reason, finally,
than that it didn't go right.
Ours is the story of how
is became *was* and *was* became

wasn't, became *no,*
became *not.* The story of
our almost girl, our *might've been.*
The doctor closed his chart
and said, "I'm not seeing what
I should see." The smallest heart
we'd ever dreamed of
wasn't moving. He couldn't
hear you. I wanted
to hate him, have this be
his fault. The room was too small
and dark and hot and
then I couldn't hear anything
either. Summer's no season

for grieving, it doesn't
satisfy, it's too sunny
and warm and everything
keeps pushing
into stalky shoots of green,
frilly leaves, pink and yellow
flowers, it just goes on
and on and on. Even the crickets
chirp away each night
as if it'll last forever
and they will too, so why not
make music, let everyone know

they're here
and loving it. You would

have loved the insect market
in Shanghai—that muddle
and crush of booths and boxes
and bins, the pull and push
of an open-air bazaar
but covered over
with scraps of tarp and tin
that let in broken
half-moons, quarter-moons
of sky so that buyers and sellers
alike hunker down,
elbow into the dingy half-light
and bug-hum of commerce.
Hawkers show off
black crickets in plastic vials,
feeding each one
an eye dropper's worth of sugar
water, the bigger bugs
(what *are* those?) squeezed into
bamboo cages, insects long

as my thumb with whipsaw
legs, serrated, iridescent black
and green, a flash of red
down the back. The dealers up
and coming, or down
on their luck, are booth-less
and table-less: they squat
on the concrete, clay pots
arranged before them,
lifting each lid to check on

the dark, shiny cricket inside—
Still there? Still ready
to fight for your life?
You would have been

an only child like me
or like so many kids in China,
those privileged
loners, and so many here
adopted from there,
preparing now
for bat mitzvahs or dyeing
Easter eggs pink and orange,
carpooled to weekend
calligraphy and lion dance
classes by blond dads,
moms who teach poli sci
at Columbia, wondering—
loved but still curious, loved

but confused by the odd
escapes that shape
our lives—*How on Earth*
did I ever wind up here?
You would have been
an only child like me, alone
but not lonely
most of the time, lost
a little, but mostly
okay with it all—
the living inside your mind,
I mean, the wandering
through the woods,
those half-remembered, half-
imagined woods—

and laughed at this old man:
"My *dad?*" you'd say. "How
weird," you'd say—every
sentence a question
shiny with italics—"the things
he *says?*" Wary teen, how
you'd laugh with your friends,
of whom you'd have many
from all over our shrinking
world—smaller still
by the time you got here
and grew up and started talking

like this. "Specs? Records?
Cassettes?" You'd laugh at this
old man from an older world
already mostly gone,
already over with, the way
the music I love was played
by people dead now for decades,
like Joe Oliver, who shouted
and rasped and rushed
golden notes through his cornet,
his many mutes—derbies
and plungers and bottles and cups—
making a *wah-wah* wheezing
singing crying human voice
out of his hot breath,
so sad and sweet for so long
until his teeth rotted and it hurt
too much to play. He ended up

a janitor in a Georgia pool hall
and died too young,
busted and broke, buried—

How on Earth?—here
in the Bronx, in Woodlawn
Cemetery, not far from Shakespeare
Avenue, where I would take you
to see the green street sign.
And Thelonious Monk,
who got so rundown and sick
he slipped away across the river
to Englewood and told
his sister, "I just don't feel
like playing anymore."
Not even "'Round Midnight,"
not even "Crepuscule
with Nellie," the song he made
for his wife and always
played note for note,
just as he wrote it. So he didn't
touch a key, not ever
again, his mind and his piano
slowly filling up

with dust. Out in
Ewen Park now, the trees
one shade darker
than the sky, the fireflies
play hard to get
beneath the moon. They blink
on and off, on
and off. They telegraph us
their secrets—

over here

over here

—with their green
glow-in-the-dark bellies.
When we moved here, Lily and I
stopped in surprise
to watch those here and gone
and here again

tiny lights I remembered
from childhood and had never
seen before in the city,
though soon we realized
they appear here all summer.
Someone told me
it's their mating call
though I never looked it up
to see if that was true

and now we walk right by
in our hurry to get home.
But since this is all
just imagining anyway, reckless
careening around curve
after curve, no brakes, eyes
closed, and since I can hear it now—
your voice, your sweet laugh
that hasn't hurt anyone—
I want to stop here, mid-
sentence, and open my eyes
so I can look at you:

my slight girl, tall and awkward
in glasses, uncertain-seeming
(like your mother) and too
quiet sometimes (like me)

so that people who don't
know you, not really, try to
finish your sentences, rush you
along, even though you're nearly
fifteen, as if they've got you

figured out. But you're steely
underneath—that crease
between your eyebrows
the giveaway you're sure
of what's what without needing
to say so. Your long brown hair
lightens to honey in summer,
mysterious chemistry of pool water
and sunlight, something
I would've never figured out

the *how* of and been happy
just to see and love and not try
to explain. Curious about anything
with legs or wings—lizards,
moths and caterpillars, toads, birds,
the broken eggs beneath the oak
that *do* require some explanation—
you're only six, I see
now, sharp-eyed and skeptical
before you have any reason
to be: no one's died yet

you know. You squint when
you smile, you may
need braces, you have a cloud
of freckles across each
cheek, you keep
losing one red mitten

and finding it again, you say
snowflakes taste
like little rivers when
they fall on your tongue

and then a door slams shut
on that other life. What

woke me up? Somewhere
a bell rings. Another door

slams: a literal door now,
wooden and loud. Someone

grinds coffee—*whir, whir*—
lets the water run until it's cold

enough. Lights go on up
and down the hill, first one

and then another and then
another. God *bless* it—

as my father used to
say, angry but not wanting

to swear because
there was a child there—

another day gets going.
What else can we do

but get going too?
So I'm here. Still trying to

make what happens make
some kind of sense.

God bless it, I think, this
painful imagining

and then the cold light
we wake to once more.

What comes after:
we keep wondering when

will that start? So here's
the rest of the story I want you
to hear: of course we didn't
buy any crickets. But as we haggled
over the price of a cricket case,
small as a deck of cards
with a sliding lid
of curlicued wood over
a plastic window so you can see

your cricket sitting there
(legs angled in, antennae
aquiver), the cricket-seller—
a young woman who knows
how old, eighteen, twenty-
eight? She was someone's
daughter, her ball cap
pulled low, her ponytail
sprouting out the back—
offered to throw in
a free cricket to seal the deal.
Perfect souvenir

from a faraway world:
I thought I'd keep my case
pocketed like a worry stone
I could rub to wear away
my worries. I'd keep it
empty, but at the ready.
As I held it and turned it over,
looked at it and tried to decide—
too expensive, I thought, too
wonderfully useless
for me, though if I said no

when would I ever
have the chance again?
—an old man squeezing
through the crowd stopped
and turned back. Two
bent and wiry hairs stuck out
of his cheek: a long life,
this means in China, if
he doesn't pluck them. He said
something to the woman
and pulled from his pocket—
like a perfect moment's

magic trick—his own
identical case. He slid back
the cover to show me
his mechanical-looking cricket.
His smile said he appreciated
the coincidence, this chance
to show it off—I couldn't tell you
how, but I could tell
his cricket was a prized one,

a scrappy survivor.
He was happy in the right now
of this moment. He loved
his cricket even if
or maybe just because
they only ever live a few weeks
and so, unable to fall back asleep,

I step out
empty-handed now
to look once more at the moon.

Three Deer Beneath
the Autumn Moon

Dusk in August—
which means nearly
nine o'clock here, an hour
south of home, deep
in the heart of central
Jersey—and the deer
step out to graze
the backyards. They tear
each yellowy red
tulip cup, munch up
rhododendrons
and azaleas. Fifty
years of new houses
have eaten into
their woodland, leaving
only this narrow strip
of trees along the trickly
stream that zigzags
between Route 9
and Lily's mom's
backyard. The deer rise
from the mist, hooves
clicking on asphalt, a doe
and a buck, his antlers
like a chandelier.
Sometimes a doe and two
fawns. Or else we see
just the white flags
of their tails bobbing away
into the dark. In theory
the DNR should come
catch them, let them go
where it's still
forest, still possible to live
as they were meant to.

But these days
there's no money
for that. And people keep
leaving out old bread,
rice, stale cookies, or else
plant more delicious flowers.
"Mei banfa,"
my mother-in-law says:
Nothing can be done.
Seeing them in
the distance—that distance
we can't close
without them shying
and turning and skittering
down Dickinson Lane
or bounding
over a backyard fence—
I try to imagine
they're messengers
come back to tell us
their stories, any news
of the lost or what
comes next, though
if they could say
anything, they would
probably say, *Go away.*

This is the story of
what's missing, a space
one can see only
because we've filled in
everything around it:
keyhole I peer through
to what I can't hold,
little hole in my heart
where the air leaks out,
little no more, no luck or way
or how. I write *one*
as if that distance
softens the ache, makes it
easier to know this
hurt, as if *one* meant
something other than
a person who's alone,
who's lonely. *One* means
I'm by myself. This *one*
is me. Autumn now

and I wish I could read you
these old Chinese poems
I love, which rarely use
the word *I* (or *Wo,* to say it
in Chinese: "Wo ai ni"
means *I love you,*
which I do). So it's only
because of an understanding
built up over hundreds
of years, the common warp
in which the weft
of each new poem
was woven, that anyone
who reads these poems—

whether in the original Chinese
like Lily's mom or
the English translations
I get by on—and so hears

the last yellow leaves
clinging to the black branch
creak and moan
as the wind sweeps through

or sees how

a swan circles the slate-gray lake,
searching for her mate

knows these poems
are really about Lao Wen
and his own inner weather,
his griefs and worries, heart-
break, illness, someone dear
but far from him
he will never see again
even though he hardly ever
shows his face in them.

Dear almost—

Dear keyhole I squint through
to see that other life—

Pinpoint of light
that life revolves around—

Dear heart I can't hear
anymore, alone

in the woods. I walk back
into the past, last spring's
leaves crumbling
underfoot. It's September,
deep in the season of decay
and forgetting,
but I want to hold on

to everything. Look
how that gray squirrel
socks away acorns
to make it through winter.
How does he remember
where they're all hidden?
And above us, delicate
brown nests woven
into high-branching vs, dark
against the stark pale sky.
Most birds make new ones
each year, so these are left

to rot. They'll be gone
by spring when the birds return.
They're closing up shop.
They're packed and prepped
for the long caravan south.
How do they do it?
"Get started," my father
would say. "Then keep

going." This morning
I don't want to remember,
it's not in keeping
with the season, which repeats
what's closest

to hand like a mockingbird:
let go, let go. In this cold
field I keep turning over
stones, looking for

what? And when I stop
to answer it snags me,
this hurt like a burr
hooked in the haunch
of a deer: I carry it with me
all day. I think of you still,

so *still,* and not there anymore
in that dark room,
though I ought to know
better, though I feel
the tiny light I cup
deep inside me gutter
and go out. "It's strange,"
Lily says when
I come home, "and un-
satisfying, isn't it?
To hurt like this for someone

we never met?" She turns
off the water, wipes her hands
with the yellow towel.
"But here we are, hurting for
someone we never met."
I think what we've lost

is imagination—the soft glimmer
of possibility, that hum
in the belly (this part I don't say
out loud), the lightness

I remember feeling each day
during that little while
when sarcasm and irony
and even the last bit of bitterness
had all fallen away
so that it felt like gravity
had been dialed down just for us.

Would music scare off deer? "Works
on bad boys," says Harry Chu.
At the Wawa on Wickatunk
Road, Harry cranks up the classics
to keep teens from hanging out
out front. "*Loiterers.*" They used to
drop cigarette butts, soda cans,
crinkly bits of shiny cellophane.
"Bad for business." But now it's me

who lingers, windows down, foot
on the brake, to hear the wavery sigh
of the erhu over the rush of passing
cars, snow sliding off pine boughs
as "Spring Comes to Xi Hu"—wrong

season—or the yangqin's plinks
and twinkles as "The Autumn Moon
Rises over Pearl River." Twangy
splash of the pipa over oil-dotted
blacktop. Yangqin's bright ripples
against storefront glass. So what

would keep the deer away?
"Spray coyote urine around those
rhodies and azaleas," Harry tells me.
"You can buy it online, but what
the heck, I ought to carry it here.
Or save money—piss on them
yourself. You'll keep me away too."

After the earthquake, the tsunami,
after the villages washed away
and the reactor exploded and couldn't

be cooled, after it became too much
to count the lost, Emperor

Akihito entered the television
studio to speak to his people. *Keep
going,* he said. *You must see tomorrow.*

He sat at a bare table. He sat before
a paper screen in his dark suit, a sharp

part in his thick hair, and looked
straight into the camera. But he spoke
in a courtly language most viewers

in Japan couldn't understand.
We switch off the TV, head for the subway.

We're late, but sneak into our family
circle seats after the overture.
We strain to follow along

as a deep-voiced Spaniard brings
the first Chinese emperor back to life

for more than three hours
by singing in English. Where are we
again? And there's this, too,

for the record: in night school
at The New School, struggling to pick up

a little Mandarin—"Ni mama zai ja ma?
Hen hao"—I keep remembering
more high-school French.

Deng Laoshi ("First lesson is this
means *Teacher Deng*") wants to know

where my mind's wandered off,
but I can't help caressing these keepsakes
I'd thought gone for good: *maillot*

de bain, boucle d'oreille. The world slips
away sometimes, and sometimes

slips back, between words. *Je ne joue pas
du piano. Je parle chinois
un peu.* French sounds like cursive,

English like printing, Chinese like
the solid whump-thump of a hand-cranked

printing press, but Japanese—
whether it's the emperor in his old-
fashioned, embroidered prose

or a blue-haired kid hawking iPads
and iPods under the bright lights

of the Ginza—Japanese sounds
like the sweep of a brush dipped in dark
ink, a fast foaming river, water

birds rising on glossy black
wings, like the rush and clack of hooves

on stone. Back in Japan on the shrine
island of Miyajima, deer wander the alleys
and lanes, eat whatever they want,

tame as dogs. Messengers of the gods,
they're called. Narrow hipped,

white spotted. With damp
black noses, bright dark eyes. I wanted to
pet one—they're not much bigger

than big dogs and walk right up to you—
but thought of lice and ticks and

backed away. This was ten years ago,
the maples ablaze with feathery red leaves.
Lily and I wore ourselves out

hiking up and down Mount Misen,
then stumbled back to the landing

hunger-drunk and numb. Already dark
now, late and getting later, and because
we sat inside the ferry's cabin,

out of the cold but away from
a window, enveloped in engine hum

and that constant rocking, we couldn't feel
the boat moving. Didn't understand
the captain's terse words over the PA

or recall what a quick trip it was
from Hiroshima to this island

or remember how the ride home—
any ride home—always feels
shorter than the ride there, and so

we rode the ferry all the way around
and stepped onto the jetty

on Miyajima again. We were so tired
we did this twice, like a bad
joke, a bad dream, though the deer

welcomed us each time—bounding
forward on skinny legs, clicking hooves,

nosing our pockets to sniff out
any salty snacks—as if they had never
seen us before, or seen us

only once, long ago, and felt so glad
that now, at last, we had finally arrived.

Back in the scruff
of western Jersey
I watch the hunters in blaze-
orange vests hurry off
into the woods, worried
and whiskery, zoomed in
in my binoculars. Must be true
that deer are color
blind, so this Day-Glo orange
is for us, or really
them, the hunters, to keep
from shooting each other,
since most people
aren't color blind.
Which makes me think
of the buzz-cut soldiers
guarding Grand Central
I pass each morning
heading to work: strange

how it's no longer strange
to see them there, M-16s slung
over shoulders, decked out
in desert camouflage.
Commuters stream past
and shiver or look twice
or don't, not anymore, don't
even slow down. The point is
for them *not* to blend in
but to stand in
plain sight freaking out
aspiring terrorists twice
as much as they freak us out.
As for hunting, I'd do it too

if I could leave the guns
behind and not wear orange
and know that for one day
no one would die.
I'd walk into the woods
and lose myself
awhile, alone and not
lonely. I'd slip away between
the trees the way the light
does. We lose
two more minutes
each day—

November bleak and dark,
cold old tail-end of the year.
In the distance of a field
all browns and grays,
brittle leaves, stones and fallen
branches, it'd be my turn
to disappear. You'd have to
look closely if you were here,

raise a hand to shade
your eyes, and then your mind
might wander away
and you'd remember how
I told you in a different place,
a different field, years and years
before, that the red deer—
This was in England, this was
long, long ago—
was once called a hart.

Think of a place where
you could pray, a place to be alone
together, that's what
we've been told
we need. So: a cabin to camp out
in. The roof's corrugated
tin, there's water we pump

by hand and each day a scoop
of bean curd on brown rice.
Touch of ginger, touch
of salt. The monks
are patient: they make
their own sandals from old tires
and understand
that I *don't* understand
and so don't bother talking
to me. Silence is a blessing

but how could we ever
go there? I work all week
in a Midtown office
tower: emails, spreadsheets,
conference calls. All day I gaze
into the laptop's glow,
tap the mouse.
By night my fingers tingle.
Still we try to pray.
"Something simple, I need
something simple, God

damn it," she says—this is
Lily; this is morning,
or still night?—"something
that goes right. There's

a piece of me that's
missing. I almost didn't
know she was there
but she was there and now
she's gone." And there's

nothing I can do
except arrange
these careful words

so we can feel
the shape they make—
A ladder? The dock

leading us back
once more to the island?
—and hold on tight.

So give me a sign if
you're out there, if you're
the light swaying, swinging
between trees, that light
growing faint, drifting deeper
into the shadowy woods,
if you're that pale glow

between the elms and alders.
What star do you steer by?
Where are you going?
Tell me you can hear this
if that's you who pauses
beside a ragged oak,
head cocked to one side
like a doe, light bouncing back
from your dark eyes,
if that's you moving under
starlight and moonlight,
waiting for a gauze of cloud
to dim the world

so you can slip away
once more. Tell me, are these
your footprints I find
in the morning in the dark
wet earth, faint traces
in the muck and loam
that slowly fill with water?

The Day Winter
Gives Way

Now it's December
and snow over
everything: even this
dirtiest city—
cellophane bits skittering
in the wind, crushed
paper cups, drops
of motor oil
along 231st Street—
gets whited out. Which is

why I love
winter: one big do-
over. "Start
from scratch," my mother
would say: no
cross-outs, no mistakes
yet. Everything's
promise and possibility
for a full

five minutes. Which can be
a lifetime.
"Take as much time
as you need,"
the technician told us,
backing out of the dim
sonogram room—
the screen
had silently switched off—

but after five minutes
she came back
knocking:
other couples needed

their news—
good or bad or
try again. It was time.

I love the inconclusiveness
of snow: how it
hushes us, forgetfuls
us, dampens
and blankets and blanks.
It might mean
anything. Blank and
we don't know
what's under,
blank and for five minutes
all the world

now, all the words now,
covered over: all
forgotten, all forgiven.
Even my footprints,
feeble proof
I was here, disappear
in the *hush-shush-shush* as

snow falls
so softly now
on snow.

Late afternoon and already
dusk inks in the gaps
between trees, the thick swag
of pine boughs heavy with snow.
I'm alone and with you
always—little weight I swing

onto my shoulder,
my worry stone, my rosary
bead come loose from your string.
I walk until I feel the cold
through my boots.
I walk and keep coming back

to that miner's helmet,
the keyhole of its fading light.
All they found. And all they—
the other *they*, the *they*
I hate to imagine and can't help

imagining—left behind.
Where did they go? Do you
decide, when all hope's
flickered out, to turn around
and walk back deeper
into the mine?

"Life is fucked
up and complicated
and ugly," the old
movie director
says, sitting in
the dark.
"The editing suite
isn't." But he's seen
so much—born
in Germany, lost
or given up,
anyway an orphan
brought to
America, scrawny
and wordless,
caught a rare
disease and lost

all his hair, even
his eyebrows—
I mean lost
forever—but went on
to be funny, direct
plays, make
movies, *films*, make
a name for
himself (an American
name, one he
made up), so many
awards, even
recognized
on the street. He
stayed at The Plaza
for decades.

Ate room service twice
a day. And now

here he is
on TV—this must be
from years ago—
his wig shaggy, un-
even, hands
busy with a lighter
and cigarette and
he looks
right into the camera
and says it all
in one
smoky exhale:
"Thank God I get
to choose
what to include and
just leave it—
leave all this other mess
right there
on the fucking floor."

Because we can't control
the heat in this old apartment

one window stays open
half an inch all winter.
Outside everything's freeze-

framed, but in here we're green
and steamy. On shelves,

side tables, on windowsills
and bookcases: wherever there's
a surface there's a plant.

They finger out new shoots—
stems spaghetti-thin,

leaves like hands or hearts.
Don't we love when things grow
and keep growing? Like one

of those stories: Once a girl
buried a golden seed in the dark

wet earth. She leaves
and forgets and when she returns
a green stem lifts into the sky.

Unless she doesn't come back.
Then there's no story: time

stops. In here, it's always
summer. Lily works in fresh soil:
trims, waters, stakes, ties back.

"Her babies," her mother says
just once. Succulents sit close

to the windows in terracotta pots:
some we must turn each day,
they turn so quickly to the light.

One's squat and square,
stippled like a lizard's head.

And here's oxalis, which opens
each morning: a cloud
of purple bow ties. Goldfish

plant, money tree. The jade keeps
sticking out more plump thumbs.

"If you want a cactus to grow
stop watering it, stick it
in a cold room—hey, just forget

about it," Harry Chu advises.
But we like to see them each day.

This one—serrated leaves,
stems stiff as toothpicks—
grew from a seed

we dropped in a pot once
to see: what would happen?

New Year's Day—
I think of Kobayashi Issa,
who thought about it too.

Cusp of another year—
creak of the hinge
as a door swings open.

The old here-we-go-again of January:

New Year's Day, Issa wrote.
Everything's in bloom. I feel about average.
Did he mean average as in so-so
or like *Everything's in bloom*
and here I come now, blooming too? Like that
lizard-head succulent that flowers
once a year? It lasts a day.

So quickly now, while my pencil's sharp:

New Year's Day—
tinsel-glitter in the pines
set out with the trash.

New Year's Day—
in the shop window
white mittens half-off.

New Year's Day—
nearly clear broth
in a pale-blue bowl.

Issa lost a daughter. And wrote
a haiku for her, though
like the Chinese poets he isn't

in it. Neither is she. *The world
of dew,* Issa wrote, *is
the world of dew. And yet, and yet—*

But if they leave everyone out
what's left? Grief does
end eventually, doesn't
it? We cry so much we feel
thirsty. Lily did. I kept
bringing her cups of cold water.

This morning the neighborhood
kids are loud and out
sledding. They're grabbing
their last chance for it this season.
Lily and I walk unplowed Netherland
Avenue, looking down
the long hill, and so they're small
to begin with and only

get smaller as they sled away.
Spied through skinny trees
they look like the country folk
in a Brueghel painting,
all those Flemings cavorting
and falling down, skating
and laughing and sawing
fishing holes in the bright face
of a frozen lake—or frolicking

on the ice-crusted swells
of this big Bronx hill: a dozen
decked out in red and yellow
scarves, furry earmuffs or hoods
up, with mismatched gloves, puffy
down jackets green and blue,
and look at that orange saucer sled
like a setting sun. From here

the hubbub is wordless
but punctuated with laughter.
From here they look blurry
as if seen through thumb-smudged
glass: something loved and held
too often and so now kept
out of reach. They're out

of focus when what I've tried
so hard to do is keep everything
in focus, crisp and sharp

as this blue jay zipping
down to the branch beside me:
blue crest, white breast,
beak black and open, tensed
little fist of a body
like a splash of bright paint
on the quivering branch,
his *how-de-do?*
morning call and quick as that
he's gone. They're mean,
I remember someone saying—
Harry Chu? But is that
true? It calls back

half a memory: a different
bird, different branch. That flicker
and flash of light, the way
she wouldn't let go
of what? Something
bright in her beak and I held
my breath to see—*stay*
still—what would happen.
Then the gear catches,

this March day revs up again.
My glasses steam up
as we walk back
into our apartment building.
It's simple: I want you
to see what I see.
But what's missing here is

what's always missing:
more time. These kids
know joy lasts
as long as the snow.
Not long. It's sputtering out
already, one lone flake
drifting down. And soon

it's history: just a sooty crust
behind the bus stop.
Then the crocus pokes its head
through the dirt, first one up
each spring. These days become
the past so quickly. They slip
into shadow and we forget them,
so busy with today
and today and today.

I think of you a little
less each day.
I don't want
to return
to that dark room
though I'm jolted
right back
sometimes, seeing
a girl looking out
a bus window
or holding
someone else's hand
on the subway.
I try to keep
moving. Almost time
to let you go:
knot I can't unpick,
safe I can't crack
though I've kept my ear
tight to the door,
turning that dial.
We've had our time
together. I wanted you
to see the snow.
I wanted to show you
these days, what
life is like. It scares me
I can no longer
picture your face,
which was only ever
my memory of
my imagining of
how your face
might look someday—

not enough
to hold onto.
I've had to learn to live
with this: we
didn't see you, didn't
meet you, only
knew you
were there a little while
and then
you weren't.
It's this question
I've kept
coming back to
all year: how
can I love you
without
ever knowing you?
And there's no
answer, finally,
none at all—
but I still do.

Spring again—
time to let all that comes after
finally come

but then I turn back and hear it—

snow in early spring

dusts the green shoots
poking up
from the dirt

the yellow crocus
gone
white on one side

pale buds against a pale sky
snow in early spring

the last flakes
fill the cups
of the first daffodils

flurries in early spring—

little dustings blown
against the north side
of each low thing

front stoop
back stoop
cemetery stones—

not a memory
but the echo of a memory

gone
before I could write this
        down—

but once you say *once*
a door swings open

a story begins—

        even as it falls
the snow
        turns back to rain

and yet—

        what we feel is snow
so soft so slow
        drifting down all around us

once in early spring

Notes and Acknowledgements

Thank you to the editors and readers of the journals where parts of this book were originally published, often in earlier versions: *The American Poetry Review, Chest, Connotation Press, Innisfree Poetry Journal, Lilliput Review, Ocean State Review, The Warwick Review,* and *Water-Stone Review.* "The Light that Lasts All Summer" first appeared in *Nimrod International.*

Excerpts from "Once in Early Spring" and "Three Deer Beneath the Autumn Moon" were featured online as part of the Academy of American Poets' Poem-A-Day project.

An excerpt from "Three Deer Beneath the Autumn Moon" also appeared in the chapbook *A Green River in Spring* (Autumn House Press, 2015).

The book epigraph is a quotation from Marianne Boruch's poem "Nest" from *A Stick That Breaks and Breaks* (Oberlin College Press, 1997).

The description of the Japanese emperor's television address owes a debt to Evan Osnos's article "Aftershocks" (*The New Yorker,* March 28, 2011).

The versions of haiku by Kobayashi Issa in "The Day Winter Gives Way" are adapted from *The Essential Haiku* (Ecco, 1994), edited by Robert Hass.

Thank you to the Bronx Council on the Arts and the Dorothy Sargent Rosenberg Memorial Fund for their generous encouragement. I'm especially grateful to Ava Leavell Haymon, my series editor, for her close readings and good counsel, and to Stuart Greenhouse, Leslie Harrison, and Jay Leeming, my old friends in poetry, for their thoughtful advice on early drafts. I also wish to express my continuing gratitude to Judy Deng for the Mandarin lessons and to Richard Siler, who many years ago taught me French.

This book is written to one who was lost, but it is for the two who are with me always: Lillian and Preston, my wife and son.

CPSIA information can be obtained at www.ICGtesting.com
Printed in the USA
LVOW11s1247100916

504049LV00007BA/592/P